GUDIE BOOK FOR B.COM 1ST SEMESTER ENTREPRENEURSHIP DEVELOPMENT

PART B - ENTREPRENEURSHIP DEVELOPMENT
AS PER BODOLAND UNIVERSITY SYLLABUS

ANJOY BASUMATARY

Contents

Preface

"Welcome to this comprehensive guidebook on Entrepreneurship Development. This guidebook is designed to be a valuable resource for B.COM students who are looking as a comprehensive reference book as per Bodoland University Syllabus.

Throughout the book, you will find questions and answers that will help you cover the entire syllabus. The book is organized in a systematic manner as pcr the syllabus published by Bodoland University, so that you can easily find the information you need.

I hope that this guidebook will be a valuable resource for you as you prepare for the exams. If you have any further questions or need additional help, please feel free to my mail as anjoybasumatary@ustm.ac.in

Thank you for choosing this guidebook. I hope that it helps you achieve your goals and that you find it to be a valuable resource."

Please let me know if there's something specific you would like to include or if there's anything else I can help you with.

CHAPTER I

1. What is the concept and meaning of Entrepreneurship?

Ans: The concept of entrepreneurship refers to the process of identifying, developing, and managing a new business venture with the goal of making a profit. This involves identifying a need or opportunity in the market and creating a new product, service, or business model to meet that need. Entrepreneurs are known for their ability to think creatively and take risks to achieve their goals, and they are often driven by a desire to make a positive impact on the world.

Entrepreneurship is the process of creating something new with value by devoting the necessary time and effort, assuming the accompanying financial, psychic, and social risks and receiving the resulting rewards of monetary and personal satisfaction and independence. The meaning of entrepreneurship is not just limited to starting and running a business, but also encompasses a wide range of activities and skills, such as identifying opportunities, developing and managing a business plan, assembling a team, raising capital, and building a sustainable and scalable business.

The concept of entrepreneurship is closely related to innovation, as entrepreneurs often identify new and untapped market opportunities, and create new products or services to meet those needs. Entrepreneurship is the process of taking an idea and turning it into a successful business venture, which can take many different forms.

In summary, Entrepreneurship is the process of creating something new by taking risks, identifying opportunities and bringing together a unique combination of resources to exploit them, with the goal of creating value, making a profit, and achieving personal and financial independence.

• • •

2. What is the nature of Entrepreneurship?

Ans: The nature of entrepreneurship is multi-faceted and complex, as it encompasses a wide range of activities, skills, and attributes. Some key elements of the nature of entrepreneurship include:

1. Innovation: Entrepreneurs are known for their ability to identify new and untapped market opportunities and create new products or services

to meet those needs.

2. Risk-taking: Entrepreneurs must be willing to take risks in order to start and grow their business. This includes investing time, money, and resources into a venture with an uncertain outcome.

3. Creativity: Entrepreneurs must be able to think outside the box and come up with new and innovative solutions to problems.

4. Vision: Entrepreneurs must have a clear vision for their business and be able to communicate that vision to others.

5. Resilience: Entrepreneurs must be able to bounce back from setbacks and keep going in the face of adversity.

6. Adaptability: Entrepreneurs must be able to adapt to changes in the market and adjust their business strategies accordingly.

7. Leadership: Entrepreneurs must be able to lead and inspire a team, as well as make important business decisions.

8. Flexibility: Entrepreneurs must be able to change direction as needed and be willing to pivot their business strategy if it's not working.

9. Passion: Entrepreneurs must be passionate about their business and truly believe in the products or services they are offering.

10. Tenacity: Entrepreneurs must have the drive and determination to see their business through the tough times and to keep pushing forward.

Overall, the nature of entrepreneurship is the ability to identify, create, and capitalize on new opportunities, which can take the form of new products, new markets, new technologies, or new ways of doing things. Entrepreneurs are known for their ability to think creatively, take risks and persevere to achieve their goals.

• • •

3. What are the functions and significance of Entrepreneurship ?

Ans: Entrepreneurship performs several important functions and has significant significance for the economy and society. Some of the key functions and significance of entrepreneurship include:

1. Job creation: Entrepreneurship is a major source of job creation, as new businesses often require employees to help them grow and succeed.

2. Economic growth: Entrepreneurship drives economic growth by creating new products and services, expanding markets, and increasing productivity and efficiency.

3. Innovation: Entrepreneurship encourages innovation by identifying new and untapped market opportunities and developing new products and services to meet those needs.
4. Competition: Entrepreneurship promotes competition by introducing new businesses and new products and services into the market, which can drive down prices and improve quality.
5. Social mobility: Entrepreneurship provides opportunities for social mobility by enabling individuals from diverse backgrounds to start and grow their own businesses.
6. Regional development: Entrepreneurship can help to spur regional development by providing jobs, attracting investment, and revitalizing local economies.
7. Consumer benefits: Entrepreneurship benefits consumers by introducing new products and services and by driving down prices through competition.
8. Environmental sustainability: Entrepreneurship can play a role in promoting environmental sustainability by developing new and innovative clean technologies.
9. Community development: Entrepreneurship can contribute to the development of communities by creating jobs and providing economic opportunities.
10. Personal fulfillment: Entrepreneurship can be personally fulfilling for entrepreneurs, as it allows them to pursue their passions, create something new, and achieve financial and personal independence.

Overall, Entrepreneurship is a key driver of economic growth, job creation, and innovation. It also provides opportunities for social mobility and personal fulfillment, and it can contribute to community development and environmental sustainability.

• • •

4. What are the qualities of Entrepreneurship ?
Ans: Entrepreneurship requires a variety of personal qualities and skills in order to be successful. Some key qualities of entrepreneurship include:

1. Vision: Entrepreneurs must have a clear vision for their business and be able to communicate that vision to others.

2. Risk-taking: Entrepreneurs must be willing to take risks in order to start and grow their business.
3. Innovation: Entrepreneurs must be able to think creatively and come up with new and innovative solutions to problems.
4. Leadership: Entrepreneurs must be able to lead and inspire a team, as well as make important business decisions.
5. Resilience: Entrepreneurs must be able to bounce back from setbacks and keep going in the face of adversity.
6. Flexibility: Entrepreneurs must be able to change direction as needed and be willing to pivot their business strategy if it's not working.
7. Passion: Entrepreneurs must be passionate about their business and truly believe in the products or services they are offering.
8. Tenacity: Entrepreneurs must have the drive and determination to see their business through the tough times and to keep pushing forward.
9. Problem-solving: Entrepreneurs must be able to identify and find solutions to problems that arise in the course of running a business.
10. Financial management: Entrepreneurs must be able to manage the financial aspects of their business, including budgeting, forecasting, and decision-making.
11. Networking: Entrepreneurs must be able to build and maintain relationships with key stakeholders such as customers, suppliers, investors and employees.
12. Adaptability: Entrepreneurs must be able to adapt to changes in the market and adjust their business strategies accordingly.

It's important to note that not all entrepreneurs possess all of these qualities, and some entrepreneurs may rely more on some qualities than others. Additionally, entrepreneurs can develop and improve these qualities over time.

• • •

5. What are the types of Entrepreneurship?
Ans: Entrepreneurs come in many different types, each with their own unique characteristics and motivations. Here are a few common types of entrepreneurs:

1. Small business entrepreneur: These entrepreneurs start and run small businesses, such as retail shops, restaurants, or service businesses. They

often focus on serving a local market and may have a hands-on role in the day-to-day operations of the business.

2. Scalable entrepreneur: These entrepreneurs focus on building a business that can be scaled up and replicated in multiple locations. They often focus on creating a product or service that can be easily replicated and sold to a large market.

3. High-growth entrepreneur: These entrepreneurs focus on creating a business that can grow rapidly and generate significant profits. They often focus on creating a new product or service that can disrupt an existing market.

4. Social entrepreneur: These entrepreneurs focus on creating a business that addresses a social or environmental problem. They often focus on creating a business model that can generate profits while also making a positive impact on society.

5. Solo entrepreneur: These entrepreneurs work alone and are not interested in scaling their business, they're more focused on their lifestyle.

6. Serial entrepreneur: These entrepreneurs have a track record of starting and running multiple businesses over time. They often have experience in different industries and are willing to take risks to start new ventures.

7. Franchising Entrepreneur: These entrepreneurs buy the rights to use an established business model, brand, and products and open their own franchise.

8. E-commerce Entrepreneur: These entrepreneurs operate their business primarily through the internet, and may or may not have a physical storefront.

It's important to note that entrepreneurs can possess traits of more than one type and also evolve over time. Additionally, Entrepreneurship can take many different forms, and entrepreneurs can choose to focus on different aspects of the business depending on their goals and interests.

• • •

6. What the Entrepreneurial Theories ? Explain them briefly.

Ans: Entrepreneurial theories can be broadly categorized into three main categories: social, economic, and psychological.

Social theories of entrepreneurship:

- Social Network Theory: This theory states that entrepreneurs are influenced by the social networks they are a part of, and that these networks can provide access to resources, information, and support that are essential to the success of a new venture.
- Cultural Theory: This theory states that entrepreneurship is shaped by cultural and societal factors, such as values, beliefs, and institutions, and that different cultures may have different levels of entrepreneurship.
- Institutional Theory: This theory suggests that the success of entrepreneurs depends on the support and resources provided by institutions such as government, banks, and universities.

Economic theories of entrepreneurship:

- Opportunity Theory: This theory states that entrepreneurs are motivated by the opportunity to create something new, rather than by financial gain. Entrepreneurs identify opportunities in the market and create new products or services to meet those needs.
- Resource-Based Theory: This theory states that entrepreneurs are motivated by the desire to control and acquire resources, such as money, technology, or expertise, in order to start and grow their business.
- Innovation Theory: This theory argues that entrepreneurs are motivated by the desire to create new products or services and that the success of a new venture depends on the level of innovation.

Psychological theories of entrepreneurship focus on the role of personality traits, motivation and cognitive processes in shaping entrepreneurship.

- Psychological Trait Theory: This theory suggests that entrepreneurs possess certain personality traits or characteristics, such as risk-taking, self-confidence, and locus of control, that make them more likely to become entrepreneurs.
- Self-efficacy Theory: This theory emphasizes that entrepreneurs have a belief in their own capabilities to bring about desired outcomes, through perseverance and the ability to overcome obstacles.
- Goal-setting Theory: This theory suggests that entrepreneurs have specific and challenging goals and that the pursuit of these goals leads to increased motivation and performance.

- Entrepreneurial Intention Theory: This theory explains how individuals form intentions to start a new venture by looking at factors such as attitudes, perceived control and subjective norms.

It's important to note that these theories are not mutually exclusive, and that elements of multiple theories can be used to explain the entrepreneurial process and motivations.

• • •

7. What do you mean by creativity and innovation in Entrepreneurship?

Ans: Creativity and innovation are key concepts in the field of entrepreneurship. Creativity refers to the ability to generate new and original ideas, while innovation refers to the process of turning those ideas into practical and successful business ventures.

Creativity in entrepreneurship refers to the ability to identify new business opportunities and develop new products or services. This can involve thinking outside the box and coming up with unique ideas that can be turned into successful businesses. Entrepreneurs must be able to generate new concepts, ideas or solutions that are relevant to the current market and customer needs. Creativity can also be used to improve existing products or services, or to find new ways to reach customers.

Innovation in entrepreneurship refers to the process of taking creative ideas and turning them into practical and successful business ventures. It involves creating something new, whether it's a product, service, process or business model and making it available on the market. Innovation can also involve commercializing an invention or creating a new market for an existing product.

Innovation can be of different types, such as incremental innovation (improvement of an existing product or service) or radical innovation (completely new product or service). Entrepreneurs can innovate through product innovation, process innovation, or business model innovation. Entrepreneurs must have the ability to transform their creative ideas into real business opportunities by testing them in the market, gather feedback, and improve them. They should also be able to create a business plan and strategy to successfully implement the new product or service in the market.

In conclusion, creativity and innovation are essential for entrepreneurs to create new business opportunities and to differentiate themselves from competitors. The ability to generate new ideas and turn them into successful ventures is crucial for the success and growth of any business. It's important to note that creativity and innovation are not just for startups, but also for established companies looking to stay competitive in their markets.

• • •

8. What do you mean Intrapreneurship and its impact on organisation?

Ans: Intrapreneurship refers to the process of creating new business opportunities within an existing organization. It is the act of behaving like an entrepreneur while working within a larger company, and it can have a significant impact on an organization.

Some of the positive impacts of intrapreneurship on an organization include:

1. Innovation: Intrapreneurship encourages employees to think creatively and to develop new products, services, or business models that can improve the organization's competitiveness and create new revenue streams.
2. Improved employee engagement: Intrapreneurship allows employees to take ownership of their work and to feel a sense of purpose and fulfillment. This can lead to increased employee engagement and motivation.
3. Increased agility: Intrapreneurship allows organizations to quickly adapt to changes in the market and to respond to new opportunities. This can make the organization more agile and better able to compete in a rapidly changing environment.
4. Cost savings: Intrapreneurship can lead to the development of more efficient processes and technologies, which can result in significant cost savings for the organization.
5. New revenue streams: Intrapreneurship can lead to the creation of new products, services, or business models that can generate new revenue streams for the organization.

However, it's important to note that intrapreneurship can also have some challenges for the organization, such as the lack of resources or support, the risk of employees leaving the company, and the need to balance short-term and long-term goals. Organizations must create an environment that fosters intrapreneurship, providing the necessary resources, support, and incentives for employees to take on entrepreneurial roles within the organization.

CHAPTER II

1. What do you mean by promotion of New Venture?

Ans: Promotion of a new venture refers to the efforts made by an entrepreneur to increase awareness and interest in their new business. This can include a variety of activities such as advertising, public relations, sales, and personal selling. The goal of promoting a new venture is to attract customers and generate sales.

There are several strategies that entrepreneurs can use to promote a new venture, including:

1. Advertising: This can include traditional forms of advertising such as television, radio, and print ads, as well as digital forms of advertising such as online ads, social media ads, and email marketing.
2. Public Relations: This can include building relationships with the media, creating press releases, and leveraging influencers to get coverage for the new venture.
3. Sales: This can include efforts to sell the product or service directly to customers, such as through a sales team or through e-commerce channels.
4. Personal Selling: This can include building relationships with potential customers, either through face-to-face meetings or through social media, to educate them about the new venture and persuade them to buy.
5. Networking: Entrepreneurs can build relationships with other entrepreneurs, potential customers, and other stakeholders by attending events, joining organizations, and participating in online communities.
6. Content marketing: Entrepreneurs can create valuable and informative content that can be shared with the audience in order to attract and retain customers.

It's important to note that the right mix of promotion strategies will vary depending on the specific industry, target market and the stage of the business. Entrepreneurs should also be aware of the budget they have to allocate on promotion, and should focus on the most effective ways to reach their target market.

• • •

2. What do you mean by Environmental Analysis? Explain them briefly.

Ans: Environmental analysis is the process of examining the external and internal factors that can affect an organization's performance. It involves identifying and assessing the factors in the organization's immediate environment that can have an impact on its strategy and operations.

There are two types of environmental analysis: internal and external.

Internal analysis examines the organization's internal environment, including its resources, capabilities, and limitations. This type of analysis helps organizations identify their strengths and weaknesses.

External analysis examines the factors in the organization's external environment, such as the industry, competitors, and the economy. This type of analysis helps organizations identify opportunities and threats.

Environmental analysis is an important aspect of strategic management, as it helps organizations understand the factors that can impact their performance and make informed decisions about how to respond to them.

In the context of entrepreneurship, environmental analysis refers to the process of examining the external factors that can impact the success of a new business venture. These external factors can include the overall economic climate, the competitive landscape, and the regulatory environment.

Entrepreneurs use environmental analysis to identify potential opportunities and threats that may affect their new business. By understanding the external factors that can impact their venture, entrepreneurs can make better decisions about how to position their business, what products or services to offer, and how to structure their operations.

The analysis can include industry analysis, market analysis, and competitive analysis. Industry analysis looks at the overall economic conditions of the industry the business will operate in, including trends and projections. Market analysis examines the target market for the business and evaluates factors such as size, growth, and demographics. Competitive analysis looks at the businesses that will be competing in the market and assesses their strengths and weaknesses.

Overall, environmental analysis in entrepreneurship is a vital process in the early stages of starting a new business venture, as it helps entrepreneurs identify potential challenges and opportunities, and make informed decisions about how to move forward.

• • •

3. What are the stages involved in stages in promotion of new ventures. Explain them in details?

Ans: There are several stages in the promotion of new ventures:

1. Idea generation: This is the initial stage of the promotion process where entrepreneurs identify a new business idea and conduct research to assess its feasibility and potential for success. This could involve talking to potential customers, researching the industry and market, and identifying a gap in the market that the new venture could fill. Entrepreneurs may also conduct a SWOT analysis to identify the strengths, weaknesses, opportunities, and threats associated with the new venture.

2. Business plan development: Entrepreneurs develop a detailed business plan outlining their strategy, goals, and projected financials. This plan is used to secure funding and attract potential investors. The business plan should include details such as the products or services offered, target market, marketing and sales strategies, and projected financials. It should also outline the management team and their qualifications, as well as any risks or challenges associated with the new venture.

3. Market research and testing: Entrepreneurs conduct market research to gain a better understanding of their target market, customer needs and preferences, and the competitive landscape. They may use a variety of research methods, including surveys, focus groups, and interviews. They may also conduct product testing to gather feedback and make necessary adjustments. This stage helps entrepreneurs identify potential challenges and opportunities and make informed decisions about how to move forward.

4. Brand development: Entrepreneurs develop a brand for their new venture, including a logo, slogan, and overall visual identity, to create a consistent and compelling image. This brand should reflect the business's values and mission, and it should appeal to the target market. The brand will be used in all marketing and advertising efforts, and it will help to establish the business's reputation and credibility.

5. Marketing and advertising: Entrepreneurs develop a marketing and advertising strategy to promote their new venture to potential customers

and investors. This may include advertising, public relations, and social media marketing. The marketing plan should include details about the target market, the messaging and positioning of the business, and the tactics that will be used to reach the target market.

6. Launching: Entrepreneurs launch their new venture, making it available to the public, and continue to promote it through ongoing marketing and advertising efforts. This may include a launch event, press releases, and social media campaigns. The launch should be planned and executed in a way that generates buzz and interest in the new venture.

7. Follow-up and Evaluation: Entrepreneurs track their progress, evaluate the effectiveness of their promotion efforts and make necessary adjustments. This will involve monitoring key performance indicators such as sales, customer feedback, and market share. Entrepreneurs should use this information to identify areas for improvement and make adjustments as needed.

It is important to note that these stages are not linear and entrepreneurs may revisit earlier stages as they encounter new challenges or opportunities. Additionally, the amount of time spent on each stage may vary depending on the specific circumstances of the new venture.

$\bullet \ \bullet \ \bullet$

4. What are the necessary legal formalities and documents required for setting up new venture?

Ans: The legal formalities and documents required for a new venture will vary depending on the type of business, location, and other factors. However, some common legal formalities and documents required for a new venture include:

1. Business registration: Depending on the type of business, entrepreneurs may need to register their business with the relevant government agency. This could include registering as a sole proprietorship, partnership, or corporation.

2. Tax registration: Entrepreneurs will need to register for various taxes such as income tax, value added tax (VAT), sales tax and any other taxes that may be required by the government.

3. Employer Identification Number (EIN): If the new venture will have employees, entrepreneurs will need to obtain an EIN from the Internal

Revenue Service (IRS) in the United States.

4. Licenses and permits: Entrepreneurs may need to obtain various licenses and permits depending on their industry and location. This could include a business license, health department permit, and zoning permit.

5. Intellectual property protection: Entrepreneurs may need to register trademarks, copyrights, or patents to protect their brand and any unique products or services they offer.

6. Lease or purchase agreement: If the new venture will operate from a commercial space, entrepreneurs will need to have a lease or purchase agreement in place.

7. Non-Disclosure Agreement (NDA) or Confidentiality Agreement: Entrepreneurs may need to have NDAs or Confidentiality agreements in place with employees, partners, or investors to protect any confidential information related to their business.

8. Business Insurance: Business insurance is a necessary protection for any business, it covers potential risks such as liability and property damage.

9. Employment agreements: If the new venture will have employees, entrepreneurs will need to have employment agreements in place that outline the terms and conditions of employment.

It is important to consult with a lawyer or accountant to ensure that all the necessary legal formalities and documents are in place for your specific business and location. They can help ensure that the venture is in compliance with all local, state, and federal laws and regulations.

• • •

5. What are the sources of fund for New Ventures?

Ans: New ventures require funding to start and grow. There are several sources of funding available for entrepreneurs, including:

1. Personal savings: Many entrepreneurs use their own personal savings to fund their new venture. This can be a good option for entrepreneurs who have saved up enough money to cover the start-up costs of their business. However, using personal savings can also be risky, as entrepreneurs may be putting their own financial stability at risk if the business does not succeed.

2. Friends and family: Entrepreneurs may turn to friends and family for funding, often in exchange for an equity stake in the business. This can

be a good option for entrepreneurs who have a strong personal network and are comfortable asking for financial help. However, it can also be risky, as borrowing money from friends and family can strain personal relationships if the business does not succeed.

3. Angel investors: Angel investors are wealthy individuals who invest their own money in new ventures in exchange for an equity stake. These investors typically provide funding in the early stages of a business and may also offer valuable mentorship and advice. However, the process of finding and convincing angel investors to invest in a business can be time-consuming and competitive.

4. Venture capital: Venture capital firms invest in new ventures in exchange for an equity stake, usually in businesses that have high growth potential. These firms typically provide funding in the later stages of a business, after it has proven its concept and is ready to scale. However, the process of securing venture capital can be difficult and time-consuming, as these firms are selective in the businesses they invest in.

5. Crowdfunding: Entrepreneurs can raise funds by soliciting small investments from a large number of people through online platforms such as Kickstarter or Indiegogo. This can be a quick and easy way to raise funds, but it also can be hard to reach the funding goal, since crowdfunding platforms are quite competitive.

6. Government grants: Some government agencies offer grants to new ventures, usually in specific sectors such as technology or renewable energy. However, the process of applying for and obtaining grants can be time-consuming and the competition for funding can be high.

7. Incubators and accelerators: Incubators and accelerators provide new ventures with funding, office space, and other resources in exchange for a small equity stake. This can be a great option for entrepreneurs who are just starting out and need mentorship and resources to get their business off the ground.

8. Small Business Administration (SBA) Loans: The SBA provides several loan programs that can be used by new ventures to get funding. These loans often come with favorable terms such as lower interest rates and longer repayment periods. However, the process of applying for an SBA loan can be lengthy and requires a significant amount of documentation.

9. Bank loans: Some banks offer loans to new ventures, often backed by the Small Business Administration. This can be a good option for entrepreneurs who have a good credit history and a solid business plan.

10. **Lease Financing:** This type of financing allows new ventures to obtain equipment or other assets through a lease agreement, rather than purchasing them outright. This can be a good option for entrepreneurs who need to acquire expensive assets but don't have the cash to buy them outright.

It's worth noting that different sources of funding may have different requirements and terms, such as equity stakes, interest rates, and repayment schedules. Entrepreneurs should carefully consider their options and choose the source of funding that best meets the needs of their new venture.

• • •

6. What do you mean by Venture capital. Explian the concept of Venture capital and types?

Ans: Venture capital (VC) is a type of private equity financing provided to startup companies and small businesses that are believed to have long-term growth potential. Venture capital firms invest money in exchange for an equity stake in the company and typically provide funding in the later stages of a business, after it has proven its concept and is ready to scale.

The concept of venture capital is based on the idea that high-growth potential companies, which are often too risky for traditional lenders or public markets, can generate significant returns for investors if they are successful.

Venture capital firms typically have a team of professionals who are responsible for identifying, evaluating and monitoring potential investments. They work closely with the management teams of the companies they invest in to help them develop and execute their business plans.

There are several types of venture capital:

1. Seed stage: Seed-stage venture capital is the earliest stage of venture capital funding. It is used to finance the initial stages of a company's development, such as research and development or the creation of a prototype.

2. Early-stage: Early-stage venture capital is used to finance the development of a company's products or services and the establishment of its initial sales and marketing efforts.

3. Expansion stage: Expansion-stage venture capital is used to finance a company's growth, such as increasing its production capacity, hiring additional staff, or expanding into new markets.
4. Mezzanine stage: Mezzanine-stage venture capital is used to finance a company's later-stage growth, such as preparing for an initial public offering (IPO) or acquisition.
5. Late-stage: Late-stage venture capital is used to finance a company's growth leading up to its exit, such as an IPO or acquisition.

It's worth noting that the venture capital industry is constantly evolving and these definitions may not be applicable to all cases. Also, different venture capital firms may have different investment criteria and focus on different stages of a company's development.

• • •

7. What do you mean by Venture capital finance in India?

Ans: Venture capital finance in India refers to the process of providing private equity financing to startup companies and small businesses in India that have long-term growth potential. Venture capital firms in India invest money in exchange for an equity stake in the company, and typically provide funding in the later stages of a business, after it has proven its concept and is ready to scale.

In India, venture capital firms have been playing an important role in the startup ecosystem, providing funding and mentorship to early-stage companies. This has been crucial in helping many Indian startups to grow and develop. However, in comparison to mature markets, the venture capital ecosystem in India is still in its nascent stage and is facing challenges such as lack of exits, lack of a strong legal framework, and limited access to institutional funding.

The Government of India has also been taking steps to promote the venture capital industry in India by creating a conducive environment for startups and venture capital firms. This includes policies and initiatives such as the Startup India Action Plan and the India Aspiration Fund.

It is worth noting that venture capital finance in India is a rapidly evolving field and the situation may change over time as the ecosystem matures.

• • •

8. What are the different Venture capital Financing in India?

Ans: There are several types of venture capital financing in India, based on the stage of development of the companies they invest in, the industry they focus on, and their investment strategy. Some of the main types of venture capital financing in India include:

1. Early-stage venture capital: This type of venture capital is focused on investing in startups that are in the early stages of their development, such as seed and early-stage companies. These firms typically invest in companies that are pre-revenue or have minimal revenue.
2. Growth-stage venture capital: This type of venture capital is focused on investing in companies that have a proven business model, have already reached profitability, and have a clear path for scaling their business.
3. Industry-specific venture capital: These venture capital firms focus on investing in companies within specific industries, such as technology, healthcare, or renewable energy. They may have more specialized knowledge and expertise in those sectors.
4. Geographically-focused venture capital: These venture capital firms focus on investing in companies that are based in a specific region or state in India. They may have a better understanding of the local market and business environment.
5. Corporate venture capital: This type of venture capital is provided by large Indian corporations, instead of independent venture capital firms. Corporate venture capital is an investment arm of a large company, they often make strategic investments in startups that align with their business objectives.
6. Social venture capital: This type of venture capital is focused on investing in companies that have a social or environmental impact, such as sustainable energy or healthcare for low-income communities.
7. Micro venture capital: This type of venture capital is focused on investing in very early-stage companies with small funding requirements, such as startups that are still in the ideation phase or have just launched.
8. Hybrid venture capital: This type of venture capital is a combination of two or more of the above types of venture capital, they may invest in companies at different stages or focus on different industries or regions.

It's worth noting that the venture capital financing in India is a rapidly evolving field and the situation may change over time as the ecosystem matures. Additionally, different venture capital firms may have different investment criteria and focus on different stages of a company's development.

• • •

9. What do you mean by Entrepreneurship Development Program.

Ans: Entrepreneurship Development Program (EDP) refers to a program or initiative that is designed to help individuals develop the skills, knowledge, and resources necessary to start and grow their own businesses. The focus of an EDP may vary depending on the specific program, but it typically includes training and education on topics such as business planning, marketing, financial management, and leadership.

EDP can be delivered through a variety of formats including classroom training, workshops, mentoring, and hands-on experience through internships or participation in accelerator programs. It also provide access to resources such as funding, networking opportunities, and access to market.

EDP can be beneficial for a wide range of individuals, including those who are looking to start their own business, those who are already running a business but want to improve their skills and knowledge, and those who want to work in a business-related field.

The overall goal of EDP is to help individuals develop the skills and knowledge they need to succeed as entrepreneurs, and to provide them with the resources and support they need to start and grow successful businesses.

• • •

10. Define the concept of Entrepreneurship Development Program and its objectives.

Ans: Entrepreneurship Development Program (EDP) is an initiative or program that is specifically designed to help individuals develop the skills, knowledge, and resources necessary to start and grow their own businesses. The main objective of EDP is to create an enabling environment for entrepreneurship and to provide the necessary support to potential and existing entrepreneurs.

EDP generally includes training, mentoring, and coaching, as well as access to resources such as funding, networking opportunities, and market access. It is designed to help individuals develop the key skills and knowledge required to start and manage a business, such as:

1. Business Planning: EDP helps individuals to develop a clear and comprehensive business plan that outlines their business idea, target market, competition, financial projections, and strategies for growth.
2. Marketing: EDP provides training on how to identify and target the right customers, how to create effective marketing campaigns and how to measure the effectiveness of marketing efforts.
3. Financial management: EDP focuses on providing individuals with the knowledge and skills needed to manage their business finances, including bookkeeping, budgeting, and financial analysis.
4. Leadership: EDP helps individuals to develop leadership and management skills to successfully run their business.
5. Networking: EDP provides opportunities for entrepreneurs to connect with other entrepreneurs, business leaders and experts in their field, which can be valuable for gaining access to resources, knowledge, and potential business partners.
6. Access to resources: EDPs often provide access to resources such as funding, technology, and other support services that can help entrepreneurs start and grow their businesses.

The overall objective of EDP is to help individuals develop the skills and knowledge they need to succeed as entrepreneurs, and to provide them with the resources and support they need to start and grow successful businesses. It also aims to create an entrepreneurial culture, increase the number of new and growing businesses, and promote economic development.

• • •

11. What is the importance of Entrepreneurship Development Program in India?

Ans: Entrepreneurship Development Program (EDP) plays a crucial role in the growth and development of the Indian economy. In India, EDPs are typically implemented by government agencies, educational institutions, and non-governmental organizations (NGOs) to support the development of new and existing businesses.

Some of the key importance of EDPs in India are:

1. Job creation: EDPs in India aim to promote entrepreneurship and create new business opportunities, which in turn leads to job creation and economic growth.
2. Poverty reduction: EDPs can provide opportunities for individuals from low-income backgrounds to start and grow their own businesses, which can help to reduce poverty and improve their standard of living.
3. Regional development: EDPs can be targeted to specific regions or sectors in order to promote economic development and reduce regional disparities.
4. Innovation: EDPs can encourage innovation and the development of new products and services, which can lead to increased competitiveness in the global market.
5. Skill development: EDPs help to develop the skills and knowledge required to start and manage a business, which can be beneficial for individuals both within and outside the entrepreneurial sector.
6. Access to finance: EDPs often provide access to funding and other financial resources, which can be critical for the success of new and growing businesses.
7. Networking: EDPs provide opportunities for entrepreneurs to connect with other entrepreneurs, business leaders and experts in their field, which can be valuable for gaining access to resources, knowledge, and potential business partners.

Overall, EDPs in India play a critical role in promoting entrepreneurship and economic development, which is essential for the growth of the country's economy.

● ● ●

12. What do you understand by selection of trainees?

Ans: Selection of trainees refers to the process of identifying and selecting individuals who will participate in a training program or initiative. This process typically involves a series of steps and criteria that are used to evaluate potential trainees and determine their suitability for the program.

The selection process for trainees can vary depending on the specific training program and the organization that is delivering it. However, some common steps and criteria that are often used in the selection process include:

1. Application: The first step in the selection process is often for individuals to submit an application or expression of interest, which typically includes information about their background, qualifications, and experience.
2. Screening: The next step is usually to screen the applications, which typically involves reviewing them to ensure that they meet the minimum qualifications and requirements for the training program.
3. Interviews: The selection process may also include interviews, which can be used to evaluate the suitability of potential trainees and to provide an opportunity for them to ask questions and learn more about the program.
4. Assessments: Some organizations may also use assessments such as aptitude or personality tests to evaluate the potential trainees.
5. Background checks: Organizations may conduct background checks on the potential trainees to ensure that they have no criminal record or other issues that would prevent them from participating in the program.
6. Limited places: The number of places available in the program is also an important factor in the selection process, as it may limit the number of trainees that can be accepted.

The selection process for trainees is important because it helps organizations to ensure that they are selecting the most suitable individuals for the program, which can increase the chances of success and lead to better outcomes for the trainees and the organization.

• • •

13. Explain in details the meaning of target groups?

Ans: Target groups refer to specific groups of people or organizations that an initiative, program, or campaign is primarily intended to reach and benefit. These groups are typically defined by specific characteristics such as age, gender, socioeconomic status, occupation, location, or other factors that are relevant to the initiative or program.

The process of identifying target groups typically begins with a clear understanding of the overall goals and objectives of the initiative or program. This information is then used to identify the specific groups of people or organizations that are most likely to benefit from the initiative or program.

For example, a program focused on providing entrepreneurship education and training may have different target groups depending on the specific goals of the program. Some possible target groups for such a program might include:

1. Youth: programs that focus on encouraging entrepreneurship among young people may target high school and college students.
2. Women: programs that aim to increase the number of women-owned businesses may target women who are considering starting their own business.
3. Low-income individuals: programs that aim to promote economic development in low-income communities may target individuals from low-income backgrounds who are interested in starting their own business.
4. Rural areas: programs that aim to promote economic development in rural areas may target individuals who live in rural areas and are interested in starting their own business.
5. Specific sectors: programs that aim to promote entrepreneurship in specific sectors may target individuals who are interested in starting a business in that sector.

Once the target groups have been identified, the initiative or program can be tailored to meet their specific needs, which increases the chances of success and can lead to better outcomes for the target groups and the organization.

It is important to note that target groups may change over time as the initiative or program progresses, and new information is gathered. The organization should regularly assess the progress of the initiative or program and adjust the target groups accordingly.

• • •

14. Briefly outline in details about the Courses contents in Entrepreneurship Development Program?

Ans: The courses contents in Entrepreneurship Development Program (EDP) can vary depending on the specific program and the organization that is delivering it. However, some common topics that are often covered in EDPs include:

1. Business Planning: EDPs generally include training on how to develop a comprehensive business plan, which includes details about the business idea, target market, competition, financial projections and strategies for growth.
2. Marketing: EDPs often provide training on how to identify and target the right customers, how to create effective marketing campaigns, and how to measure the effectiveness of marketing efforts.
3. Financial management: EDPs typically include training on how to manage business finances, including bookkeeping, budgeting, and financial analysis.
4. Legal and regulatory compliance: EDPs often cover the legal and regulatory requirements that businesses need to comply with, such as taxes, licenses, and permits.
5. Operations management: EDPs may also provide training on how to manage the day-to-day operations of a business, including inventory management, supply chain management, and production planning.
6. Leadership: EDPs often include training on leadership and management skills, which are essential for successfully running a business.
7. Innovation and creativity: EDPs may also provide training on how to develop creative and innovative thinking, which can help entrepreneurs to come up with new ideas and solutions.
8. Networking: EDPs often provide opportunities for entrepreneurs to connect with other entrepreneurs, business leaders and experts in their field, which can be valuable for gaining access to resources, knowledge, and potential business partners.
9. Access to resources: EDPs often provide access to resources such as funding, technology, and other support services that can help entrepreneurs start and grow their businesses.
10. Mentorship and coaching: EDPs may also include mentorship and coaching from experienced entrepreneurs and business leaders, which can provide valuable guidance and support throughout the program.

Overall, EDPs cover a wide range of topics that are essential for starting and running a business. The curriculum of the program is designed to provide a comprehensive understanding of the entrepreneurship and to develop the key skills and knowledge required to start and manage a business.

• • •

15. Explain the measurement of effectiveness of Entrepreneurship Development Programs?

Ans: The measurement of effectiveness of Entrepreneurship Development Programs (EDP) is the process of assessing the performance and impact of the program in achieving its goals and objectives. The measurement of effectiveness is important to determine the program's impact, its efficiency and its effectiveness.

There are several methods that can be used to measure the effectiveness of EDPs, including:

1. Outcome measures: This method involves measuring the specific outcomes or results of the program, such as the number of new businesses started, the number of jobs created, or the increase in revenue for existing businesses.
2. Process measures: This method involves measuring the activities and processes of the program, such as the number of training sessions conducted, the number of participants in the program, or the number of mentoring sessions provided.
3. Impact measures: This method involves assessing the broader impact of the program on the community or society, such as the economic impact, the social impact, or the environmental impact.
4. Participant's feedback: This method involves gathering feedback from participants in the program, such as their level of satisfaction with the program, the skills they acquired and the effectiveness of the training.
5. Follow-up studies: This method involves conducting follow-up studies to assess the long-term impact of the program on the participants and their businesses.
6. Return on investment (ROI) analysis: This method involves calculating the financial return on the investment made in the program.

Combining different methods can provide a more comprehensive picture of the effectiveness of the program. The selection of the methods depends on the goals and objectives of the program, the resources available and the data collection capabilities.

Overall, measuring the effectiveness of EDPs is an important aspect of program evaluation and it helps to identify areas for improvement and to determine the program's impact and sustainability.

● ● ●

16. What are the institution involved in promotion of Entrepreneurship Development Programs in India?

Ans: In India, there are several institutions involved in the promotion of Entrepreneurship Development Programs (EDP). Some of the key institutions include:

1. National Small Industries Corporation (NSIC): This is a government-owned organization that provides a wide range of services to small and medium-sized enterprises (SMEs), including EDPs, financial assistance, technology transfer and marketing support.

2. National Skill Development Corporation (NSDC): This is a government-funded organization that aims to promote skill development in India and it also provides various EDPs to individuals and enterprises.

3. Small Industries Development Bank of India (SIDBI): This is a government-owned development financial institution that provides financial assistance, refinance and other support services to SMEs and also EDPs.

4. National Bank for Agriculture and Rural Development (NABARD): This is a government-owned development bank that provides financial assistance and support services to rural and agricultural businesses, and also provide EDPs.

5. Indian Institute of Technology (IITs) and Indian Institute of Management (IIMs): These are premier educational institutions in India that offer EDPs, training, research and consulting services to entrepreneurs.

6. National Entrepreneurship Network (NEN): This is a network of organizations that aims to promote entrepreneurship and provide support services to entrepreneurs, including EDPs.

7. State Financial Corporations (SFCs) and State Industrial and Investment Corporations (SIICs): These are state-level institutions that provide financial assistance, refinance and other support services to SMEs and also EDPs.

8. Incubators and Accelerators: There are many private and government-funded incubators and accelerators that provide support services to entrepreneurs, including EDPs, mentoring, networking and access to funding.

These institutions play a vital role in promoting entrepreneurship and supporting the development of new and existing businesses in India, by providing EDPs, funding, mentorship and other support services.

CHAPTER III

1. Explain in details about Role of entrepreneurs in socio-economic development in India?

Ans: Entrepreneurs play a critical role in socio-economic development in India by creating jobs, driving innovation and economic growth, and promoting social and economic mobility. Some of the key ways in which entrepreneurs contribute to socio-economic development in India include:

1. Job creation: Entrepreneurs create jobs by starting and growing new businesses. This not only provides employment for individuals, but it also contributes to economic growth and development.
2. Economic growth: Entrepreneurs drive economic growth by starting and expanding businesses, which can lead to increased productivity, innovation, and competitiveness in the global market.
3. Poverty reduction: Entrepreneurship can provide opportunities for individuals from low-income backgrounds to start and grow their own businesses, which can help to reduce poverty and improve their standard of living.
4. Regional development: Entrepreneurship can be promoted in specific regions or sectors in order to promote economic development and reduce regional disparities.
5. Innovation: Entrepreneurs are often at the forefront of innovation, developing new products and services, and finding new ways of doing things. This can lead to increased competitiveness in the global market.
6. Social mobility: Entrepreneurship can provide opportunities for individuals to improve their socio-economic status and achieve upward mobility.
7. Community development: Entrepreneurship can also contribute to the development of the community by creating jobs, generating economic activity, and providing goods and services to the community.
8. Environmental sustainability: Social-entrepreneurship can also promote environmental sustainability by creating businesses that are environmentally friendly and sustainable.

Entrepreneurship plays a key role in socio-economic development in India by creating jobs, driving innovation and economic growth, and promoting social and economic mobility. It is important to have a conducive environment and support system to promote entrepreneurship in India, which can help to achieve sustainable and inclusive economic growth.

• • •

2. Explain the role of entrepreneurs in export promotion in details?

Ans: Entrepreneurs play a vital role in both export promotion and import substitution. In Export promotion, entrepreneurs identify new export opportunities, develop new products and services, and enter new markets. They conduct market research to identify new export opportunities, such as new products, services, and markets that are in high demand. Entrepreneurs also develop new products and services that are tailored to the specific needs of export markets, and create a strong brand and marketing strategy to promote their products and services in export markets. They also develop distribution and logistics strategies to effectively get their products to export markets, and comply with regulations, such as product labeling, packaging, and certification requirements.

On the other hand, in Import substitution, entrepreneurs identify opportunities to produce goods and services domestically that were previously imported. They conduct market research to identify opportunities for import substitution, and develop new products and services that can substitute imports, such as developing new technologies, improving production processes, or creating new products that are tailored to the domestic market. Entrepreneurs also make connections with other businesses, trade organizations, and government agencies to gain access to information, resources, and support for import substitution.

Some of the key ways in which entrepreneurs contribute both to export promotion and import substitution include:

1. Market research: Entrepreneurs can conduct market research to identify new export opportunities, such as new products, services, and markets that are in high demand.
2. Innovation and product development: Entrepreneurs can develop new products and services that are tailored to the specific needs of export markets.

3. Networking: Entrepreneurs can make connections with other businesses, trade organizations, and government agencies to gain access to information, resources, and support for exporting.
4. Distribution and logistics: Entrepreneurs can develop distribution and logistics strategies to effectively get their products to export markets, such as using freight forwarders, customs brokers, and other service providers.
5. Compliance with regulations: Entrepreneurs must comply with all regulations and standards that apply to the export of their products, such as product labeling, packaging, and certification requirements.
6. Branding and marketing: Entrepreneurs can create a strong brand and marketing strategy to promote their products and services in export markets.
7. E-commerce: Entrepreneurs can use e-commerce platforms to reach global customers and to sell their products and services online.
8. Strategic partnerships: Entrepreneurs can form strategic partnerships with other businesses, organizations, and government agencies to gain access to new export markets and to leverage their resources and expertise.

In summary, entrepreneurs play a vital role in export promotion by identifying new export opportunities, developing new products and services, and entering new markets. They can also develop distribution and logistics strategies, comply with regulations, create a strong brand and marketing strategy and form strategic partnerships to leverage their resources and expertise.

• • •

3. Explain in details how Entrepreneurial Performance and Growth can be measured?

Ans: Entrepreneurial performance and growth can be measured by various methods, including both financial and non-financial metrics. The choice of metrics used to measure performance and growth will depend on the specific goals and objectives of the business.

1. Financial metrics: These metrics include measures such as revenue growth, profitability, return on investment, and cash flow. These metrics are used to assess the financial health and performance of the business.

2. Operational metrics: These metrics include measures such as productivity, efficiency, and quality. These metrics are used to assess the effectiveness of the business's operations and the ability of the business to manage its resources.

3. Strategic metrics: These metrics include measures such as market share, customer satisfaction, and brand awareness. These metrics are used to assess the effectiveness of the business's strategy and the ability of the business to achieve its long-term goals.

4. Innovation metrics: These metrics include measures such as number of patents filed, number of R&D projects, and new product development. These metrics are used to assess the ability of the business to create and implement new ideas, products, and services.

5. Social metrics: These metrics include measures such as environmental sustainability, ethical practices, and community involvement. These metrics are used to assess the ability of the business to consider the social and environmental impact of the business.

It's essential to note that the use of multiple metrics provides a more comprehensive picture of the performance and growth of the business. Additionally, regular monitoring and evaluating these metrics can help entrepreneurs to identify areas for improvement and make necessary changes to improve the performance and growth of their business.

• • •

4. What are the role of government in entrepreneurship development in India?

Ans: The government plays a critical role in promoting entrepreneurship and small business development in India. Some of the key roles of the government in entrepreneurship development include:

1. Providing access to finance: The government provides access to finance through various schemes such as bank loans, venture capital, and angel investment. This helps entrepreneurs to secure the funding they need to start and grow their businesses.

2. Providing infrastructure and facilities: The government provides infrastructure and facilities such as industrial parks, technology parks, and incubation centers to support entrepreneurs and small businesses.

3. Providing training and education: The government provides training and education programs to help entrepreneurs develop the skills and knowledge they need to start and grow their businesses.

4. Providing market access: The government provides market access to entrepreneurs through schemes such as procurement policies, trade fairs, and export promotion programs.

5. Providing legal and regulatory support: The government provides legal and regulatory support to entrepreneurs through laws and regulations that protect their rights and interests.

6. Promoting entrepreneurship culture: The government promotes entrepreneurship culture by creating awareness about the benefits of entrepreneurship and encouraging more people to start their own businesses.

7. Tax incentives and subsidies: The government provides tax incentives and subsidies to businesses to encourage entrepreneurship and small business growth.

8. Ease of doing business: The government also makes efforts to simplify the process of starting and running a business, such as simplifying regulations and reducing bureaucratic red tape.

In summary, the government plays an important role in promoting entrepreneurship and small business development in India by providing access to finance, infrastructure and facilities, training and education, market access, legal and regulatory support, promoting entrepreneurship culture and providing tax incentives and subsidies. It also makes efforts to improve the ease of doing business.